WARNING: WHAT YOU DON'T KNOW CAN KILL YOU

WARNING:
WHAT YOU DON'T KNOW CAN KILL YOU

Rhonchell W. Smith

Independently published by

Rhonchell W. Smith

2014

First Printing: July 2014

ISBN 978-1-312-37184-2

Dedication

This book is dedicated first to God, my Father who has given each of us a dream, a hope, and a future. Without these; my life would lose all meaning. It is also to every man, woman, and child who has committed his or her life to serving and loving God.

This book is for you.

Acknowledgements

I would like to thank my incredibly supportive family and friends who always see the best in me. It is because of you that this book is possible.

Contents

Introduction

Someone once asked me; "What do you think is the most important thing every believer should know to be a victorious Christian?"

The question piqued my interest because we all desire to be victorious as believers. No one accepts Jesus as Lord just to go back to life as usual. We all have goals and dreams that we wish to accomplish and most of us understand that we need God's help to make them happen. Yet for many still, there are a bevy of trials and tribulations that never seem to end. Some of us just want relief from the issues that seem to follow us wherever we go.

Many of us are still struggling as if we still don't have the everlasting life and abundant life God has promised. We attend church regularly, pray, and even fast. So why are so many of us still struggling to see the victory in Jesus?

Well, this book shall approach that question with real answers! Not just the same 'church jargon' we have heard time and time again.

There is an old adage that says; *"What you don't know won't hurt you."* But just as much of the world's brand of wisdom is contrary to God's Truth, we know this is false. Just imagine stopping to rest against a chain linked fence. Now imagine if you didn't know the fence was wired to electrocute anything that came in contact with it. You would seriously hurt yourself because you didn't know it was an electric fence. Well just as knowledge of that electric fence could save your life so is true of the Word of God. The truth is *– **What you don't know can kill you!***

"If ye continue in my word, then are ye my disciples indeed; And ye shall know the truth, and the truth shall make you free."

John 8:23

God has always desired for you to be free. But your ability to be free is only according to how much truth you know.

Many of us will accept Jesus as Lord and savior, yet never grasp the abundant life He died to bring us. That's what is killing us. It is and has always been about an intimate relationship with God the Father, but that vital relationship can only be enriched by discovering some fundamental truths in God's Word.

Through the inspiration of the Holy Spirit I have compiled three foundational principles that could potentially change your life if you are willing to adopt them. You can begin to grasp the True Gospel. What many of us are being taught is not the True Gospel. We have only heard the gospel that has been so distorted by doctrines that divide the church and the gospel that is twisted with lies that have been subtly woven in by devils, (1 Timothy 4:1). It is my desire through this book that you would no longer be deceived. God's Word is truth and those that seek Him will find Him there. You will see the Lord for who He truly is.

I believe there are three foundational principles that every Christian should adopt to live a victorious Christian life.

1. **Make God's Word top priority in your life, making it the final authority on your thoughts and actions.**

2. **Believe what God says about you.**

3. **Cooperate with the ministry of the Holy Spirit.**

Some skeptics might think this is too simplified, thinking there must be more to it than this! Well, one thing I have learned while walking with God is that people love to make a simple thing more complex!

God has gifted me with the ability to teach in a way that is simple and easy to understand. I believe that simple is not the same as stupid or ineffective. The Gospel is simple – believe in Jesus and you will be saved. But mankind has worked tirelessly to make it more mysterious. We think that the real power is in the mystique of a lengthy sermon, full of expensive words and weighty concepts.

Remember, *"God hath chosen the foolish things of the world to confound the wise; and God hath chosen the weak things of the world to confound the things which are mighty."*

1 Corinthians 1:27.

As we journey through the scriptures together, I pray you will be open to receive what God desires to show you. I pray that the Word of God would transform your thinking. I also pray that you will never be the same. Let the stronghold of false teaching be broken!

What you hold in your hands is meant to be a pocket companion that you may refer to from time to time to remind yourself of the foundational truths God has revealed in His Word. This is also meant to be a reference guide that you can reflect on and share with others to open their eyes of understanding as well.

Now let's explore these three principles in greater detail with scriptural support. I encourage you to read along with your Bible to really grasp these concepts and open the door to personal study.

#1

We must make God's Word top priority in our lives, making it the final authority on our thoughts and actions.

The Bible is the **express** word of God. It is his every communication to mankind about who He is and what He says about creation. Without God's word we are lost. We are clueless. It amazes me how many believers spend very little time in the Word. We want to know which direction to take, we have answers to why the world is so messed up….yet we seldom read the Bible!

I too am guilty of this. At times we get so busy with other things that we lose sight of our first priority; which is fellowship with God on a personal, intimate level.

How do we expect to grow as Christians if we never seek to hear what God is saying? People often pray for a greater revelation from Heaven, but so many people have yet to uncover the revelatory Word we already have! If God never speaks again, we already have everything we need to live this life because it is expressed in the Word of God. Hebrews 4:12; *"For the Word of God is quick and powerful, and sharper than any two-edged sword, piercing even to the dividing asunder of soul and spirit, and of the joints and marrow, and is a discerner of the thoughts and intents of the heart."*

It's vital to our walk that we read the Bible and let the words become rooted in our hearts.

To get a better understanding of the importance of the Word of God, we can look to Mark chapter 4 – **The Parable of the Sower.**

In this parable, Jesus teaches with the use of "word pictures" to illustrate a principle. Here, Jesus talks about 4 types of soil in which a sower planted seed. Each type of soil produced a different effect. As the sower scattered seed, some fell by the wayside and never took root because the birds devoured it. Some fell on stony ground which caused the seed to spring up before it had chance to root. Other seed fell on thorny ground which choked the plant. Other seed fell on good ground. Those seeds sprang up and yielded much fruit.

Now why is this parable important? Does Jesus want us to all run out and become farmers?

As we continue reading, we learn the meaning of this parable. Mark 4:14 says, *"The sower sows the word."*

This was powerful for me. Jesus was teaching his disciples the great mystery of the word of God. The word of God is a seed and our hearts are the soil. If we read and believe what is said, we will see the fruit of that belief.

The soil of our hearts must be prepared.

If we are like the wayside, we will quickly discard the word if we have no faith. If we are like the stony ground, we quickly receive the Word but never let it become a belief that is discerned on a heart level. Verse 17 says that the stony heart *"will endure for a time but as soon as persecution comes for the word's sake, we are offended and that word is stolen from us."*

We sometimes have a tendency to let persecution from the enemy destroy the word we have received. But know that he only came against you to try and steal the word from your heart. That word will be devoured before it can ever take root in us.

The thorny ground is a warning against letting bitterness and anger choke out the goodness of God like thorns. Verse 19 is powerful; it says, *"And the cares of this life, and the deceitfulness of riches, and the lusts of other things entering in, choke the word of God and make it unfruitful."*

Many of us find ourselves in this category where we hear the Word of God and it blesses us but, as soon as we fix our attention on the desires of our hearts (and our lack), we despise the word because we don't see it in action. We don't see God's goodness producing the wants and desires we think will make us complete. If our heart is full of lust, we cannot receive the Word of God and it becomes unfruitful.

Finally, the good ground is a heart that is open to receive the Word of God. This is what we should desire. The good ground is a heart that seeks to love God and to love His Word. This type of ground will receive the Word, let it take root, and produce a harvest time and time again.

Jesus told his disciples that if they could not understand this parable, how could they understand any parable? The condition of your heart will determine your ability to grow in God.

If your heart is full of doubt, or bitterness, or lustful desires for other things – you will struggle to learn what the Word says. But if your heart is toward God and your desire is to really know Him, the seeds of the Word will take root and dramatically change your life.

Faith and prayer are the water for that seed. The turmoil and hardship of living in a sin sick world can cause us to experience times of depression, poor health, loneliness, bitterness, poverty and despair. But if the Word of God is truly the final authority, you will choose to believe God over the bad report – no matter what things look like.

The issues I just listed are only as destructive as we allow them to be. The Word teaches us that sin has been placed under our feet. We are dead to sin. Romans 6:2, *"How shall we that are dead to sin live any longer therein?"*

Sin includes sickness, poverty, depression, and bitterness. Whatsoever is not of faith is sin. So we must let the Word of God be the True Report – that we are over-comers. It requires faith to overcome the effects of sin.

Faith must first be in the work Christ did on the cross. We must believe that he took our sins to the cross and that our old sinful nature died with him. We then believe that we are made alive through his resurrection. We are born again and made in his image with a new spirit, identical to Jesus. Sin is no longer an issue for a born again believer.

Paul encouraged the Roman church to no longer submit themselves to something that is dead. Romans 6:16, *"Know ye not that whomever you yield yourselves servants to obey, his servants you are to whom you obey; whether of sin unto death, or of obedience unto righteousness?"* You become the slave of whichever master you give yourself to. The choice is ours.

We have been deceived to think we have to endure whatever comes our way. We know that God is our answer. He is the source of relief. But sometimes we pray and it seems as though God has remained silent regarding our situation. Many of you have asked God for healing only to find little relief. Many of you are on medications for the rest of your life and you think that your relief has come in the form of a pill. But what if I told you God has already healed you? God has already come through with the exact thing you need?

If you don't believe this, it's probably because you still need to prepare the soil of your heart then discover God's Word on the situation.

Maybe you don't see any change in the situation just yet so you think God is putting you on hold. Well, it's not that God has not honored your request. Jesus said in

John 10:10; *"The thief comes only to steal, kill, and destroy: I am come that they might have life, and have it more abundantly."*

God wants you to be well! One of the greatest benefits of being born again is that we have received the very same power that Jesus had when He walked the earth. What's more, the same power that raised Jesus from the dead is in us, according to Romans 8:11.

Sadly, too many Christians never experience that power. We have been taught that to see the blessing, we have to P.U.S.H: *Pray until something happens.* We have to bombard the gates of Heaven in prayer until God moves. The only problem is that God already moved on our behalf over 2000 years ago when Jesus rose from the grave. He rose with all power in His hand. He overcame death for us. The best part is that *"if we have been planted together in the likeness of his death, we shall also be in the likeness of his resurrection."* Romans 6:5.

> **We too have the power of God in us to see the sick healed, blind eyes, opened, and the dead to rise.**

The reason we don't see the manifestation of God is because we simply don't know what His word really says. We feel helpless against the attack of the enemy. Most Christians aren't even sure if these things are of God or the devil. We've been told that God has a blessing in the midst of the trial. But this concept isn't necessarily Biblical.

James 1:17; *"Every good and perfect gift is from above and comes down from the Father of lights, with whom there is no variation, neither shadow of turning."*

This verse reveals that God is not mysteriously sending false flags of sickness disguised as a blessing. He is the Father of Lights (directly opposed to the darkness) who doesn't change or lurk in mysterious shadows.

Furthermore, James 4:7 says; *"Submit yourselves therefore to God. Resist the devil and he will flee from you."*

We have a greater power in us than the devil and all the demons of hell combined! He is in submission to us. Sickness, poverty, depression, anxiety, and anything that is below the Kingdom standard of living is SIN. We are called to resist – called to fight against evil forces - that try to steal, kill, and destroy what God has given.

It doesn't make you a bad person if you suffer with these things. But it is false to wait on God to relieve you of your suffering. **He already gave you everything you need to overcome the enemy.**

Romans 6:7, *"For he that is dead is free from sin. Now if we be dead with Christ we believe that we shall also live with him."* Death (including the curse) has no more power over Jesus and it has no more power over us.

For some readers, the things I have written may seem very radical to what you have been taught. I have been a Christian since the age of 12 and spent many years running from God because the things I was taught about God simply didn't produce good fruit. My view of God was one of a ubiquitous presence, watching me, and silently judging me. I always felt that God was farther away when I did wrong. I always thought if I wanted to stay on His good side, I had to behave myself. I was tormented in my thought life because my thoughts were ungodly. I knew I was inadequate and I couldn't meet the standard.

In my late teens, I left the church. It wasn't until my early to mid-twenties that I rediscovered a relationship with God based on grace and mercy. I found love and acceptance without having to do a lot of good deeds first. We are saved by grace *through* faith in Jesus Christ. God knew we couldn't fulfill the demands of the law by ourselves. This was the whole reason Jesus came!

I thought that this message of grace was all I would ever need. But when troubles came, I did what I had always known – I prayed for help. I never considered that I actually had any power. If I didn't receive my help, I assumed God was waiting for the right time to jump in. We used to sing a song that said; *"He may not come when you want Him but He's always on time."* I just figured God hadn't shown up to save me yet because I had more to learn in that situation. He was letting me tough it out a little longer.

But what do you do when you feel as though you have already learned the lesson but God remains silent? It causes you to doubt that He even cares. It causes you to produce a doctrine that says sometimes God says 'No.' Sometimes God allows hardship because He wants you to be a testimony for someone else. **But these ideas are as wrong as can be!**

God is not silently watching you struggle and willfully choosing not to act. He's not getting some pleasure out of watching you suffer so that He can make a grand, dramatic entrance!

The truth is, the work of Christ on the cross was so complete that God never has to do another thing for mankind. We are so infinitely blessed through the cross.

> **Everything we will ever need has been provided through Jesus Christ. Now it is our job to appropriate, *or take possession of*, the gift.**

We will dig deeper into this concept later...

I encourage you to continue reading because the true measure of a good Biblical interpretation is the fruit it bears. If what you have been learning about God has been bearing good fruit in your life, continue in that direction. But if you find yourself still feeling empty despite your efforts to live for God, then there is room for a fresh perspective.

#2

We must believe what God says about us to be true.

If we believe God's word, then we must also believe what it says about us. Many people find it easy to see God as good and perfect and infallible. God cannot sin. God never changes. *If God was wishy-washy, I certainly wouldn't follow him!*

But religion as a whole has found it difficult to believe the good things the Bible says of us – those who are born-again believers. We read the good word about ourselves and explain it away. We somehow believe the Bible is only describing how we *will* be when we get to Heaven. Or perhaps that it is only an ideal to strive for.

In fact, if a preacher told his congregation that they are perfect in God's sight and that He is perfectly pleased with us. I am confident that preacher would be booted out of that church in a hurry! The church as a whole, is much more comfortable with Old Testament condemnation preaching: *"You had better straighten up or you're going straight to hell!! You're gonna bust hell wide open for what you did! Turn or burn! God is furious!"*

We are used to being told that our sin is still an issue with God. We are taught to feel bad about ourselves until we fulfill some kind of religious duty. We must attend church regularly, pay our tithes off the gross – not the net, and pray an hour a day to cover the sins and the guilt still lurking in our closets. *Does that look like the abundant life Christ came to give?*

Not so...

Our sins are forgiven

God is not angry at mankind for sin any longer. We spend so much time telling people that sin is why God won't answer their prayers. We tell people that the sin of homosexuality is going to send them straight to hell, but these same people look the other way on those who tell *little white lies*. There are no degrees of sin with God. *God hates all sin*.

Not one of us has fulfilled God's standard yet. So how can we point fingers amongst ourselves and condemn one another to a life of spiritual impotence for sins we have committed?

Romans 5:1-2, *"Therefore being justified by faith, we have peace with God through our Lord Jesus Christ; By whom also we have access by faith into this grace wherein we stand, and rejoice in the hope of the glory of God."*

That is awesome! We have been made right with God by faith and faith produced peace with God. He is no longer at war with us because of sin. Remember that sin caused a division between us and God, but when Christ gave up the ghost, the veil of the Holy of Holies was torn in two from top to bottom, (Matthew 27:51). The torn veil was a symbol of access being granted to us. We can now freely commune with the Father one on one. No one who has sin can be in the presence of the Lord, but He no longer sees our sins when He looks at us. The Father sees the Spirit of God in you. Sin has been forgiven and doesn't need to be re-hashed in prayer before God will commune with us. It is by faith in Jesus that we are made righteous!

"Blessed are they whose iniquities are forgiven, and whose sins are covered. Blessed is the man to whom the Lord will not impute sin." Romans 4:7-8

We falsely teach that we must repent and ask for forgiveness for every sin we commit. We have to plead the blood over our latest sins in order to keep our slates clean with God. But this doesn't work. If the sins we haven't committed yet aren't forgiven yet then we can never be confident in our salvation.

If we can't be confident in the cross, we can never know the peace and joy God says we can have. If all sin has not yet been forgiven then logic states that the blood of Jesus was only powerful enough to cover sins people did over 2000 years ago. The rest of us are on our own until we learn how to pray for forgiveness. No!

Christ went to the cross one time, for all. Romans 6:9-10, *"Knowing that Christ being raised from the dead dies no more; death has no more dominion over him. For in that he died, he died unto sin once; but in that he lives, he lives unto God."*

He made salvation and righteousness available to the entire world. Romans 5:15 says that the trespass is not like the gift. It was one man's sin that brought about death but *greater* is the gift of grace brought about by Jesus Christ that extends to many.

If Adam's sin could produce death in the whole of creation, certainly the single blood sacrifice of one Jesus Christ – God in the flesh - could produce life in all creation!

We have difficulty accepting that Jesus died for the sins of all mankind. It's easier to believe He has his finger pointed at everyone who falls short. **But God is love**. He desires that all would come to repentance.

2 Peter 3:9, *"God is not slack concerning his promise, as some men count slackness; but is longsuffering toward us, not willing that any should perish but that all should come to repentance."*

The free gift of salvation is available to all but man has the freedom and responsibility to accept that free gift.

God really does see you as sinless and perfect, but to explain why, we must explore 2 Corinthians 5:17-19.

"Therefore if any man be in Christ, he is a new creature: old things are passed away; behold, all things are become new.

And all things are of God, who hath reconciled us to himself by Jesus Christ, and hath given to us the ministry of reconciliation;

To wit, that God was in Christ, reconciling the world unto himself, not imputing their trespasses unto them; and hath committed unto us the word of reconciliation."

We became a new creation at the point of salvation. It is a source of rejoicing to know that all the old baggage and junk you used to carry with you can be lifted! You have the freedom to start fresh with the Lord and turn from the ways of the past. In fact, this verse is a charge to look toward the new life you have in Jesus and to neglect the old person you used to be because that person is dead. Amen!

Because we have been made new, we are reconciled to Christ. In other words, it is like having a credit card statement in which you made several purchases but never made payments on them. The debt needs to be paid or else there is a heavy penalty.

Well, imagine that Jesus is the one who made the payment for you. He cleared your account and it has been settled. There are no more debts to be paid in your name. That is what it means to be reconciled.

Jesus made the payment for all sin. We had a serious debt and the penalty for non-payment is death.

Verse 19 says, "Christ reconciled the world unto himself, not imputing (or attributing) their trespasses unto them, and has committed unto us the word of reconciliation."

That means that the entire world has access to the same gift we have in Christ. He didn't come for the select few because we were all in need of a savior. The unfortunate fact is that many people will live their lives apart from God and die in their sins, never knowing the awesome gift that was always available to them. *What they don't know is killing them.*

As Christians, I think a large percentage of people stop at the gift of salvation. We know that when we die we get to go to Heaven, but until then life can be a little rocky. So we muddle through, give thanks in everything, and wait for the rapture.

But did you know there is an entire facet of Christianity that goes beyond your standard fire insurance?

We are one spirit

1 Corinthians 6:17, *"He that is joined unto the Lord is one spirit."*

We are One Spirit with God. That is powerful! One spirit here is translated to mean we are **identical** to God. This is crucial to understand because God is a Spirit. He does not dwell in a physical body. Unlike a physical relationship one might have with a spouse, God connects with our Spirit. That is why John 4:24 says, *"God is a Spirit; and they that worship Him must worship Him in Spirit and in truth."*

Of course we can worship God with our bodies through praise and dancing. We can kneel in reverence. We can eat right and exercise in reverence to God. But these are only outward reflections of the communion our spirit has with God the Father. **Our spirit is what God is after.**

> **If we know who we are in our spirits, we can see ourselves the way God sees us.**

Ephesians 2:18-19 says we have access by one spirit unto God and are no longer strangers and foreigners but are fellow citizens with the saints and of the household of God.

If we are one spirit with God then we are identical to Him in our spirits. We are perfect, sinless, and powerful just as Christ is. Your spirit has never sinned against God. Your spirit only praises and rejoices in the presence of the Lord continually.

The only reason believers have a hard time seeing themselves this way is because we spend too much time focusing on the flesh. We outlaw eating pork, drinking alcohol, women wearing pants, and men having heads uncovered all to get closer to God. We spend so much time trying to correct the flesh, hoping that our good works will penetrate to the heart and mind so we can finally be righteous before God.

We fail to realize that real change must occur from the inside out. The best part about being in Christ is that He has already made that change for you!

"For he hath made him to be sin for us, who knew no sin; that we might be made the righteousness of God in him."

2 Corinthians 5:21

There was an exchange we made with Jesus at the cross. He took on the form of sin for us and we took on His righteousness. Sin died with him and then he was restored to His former glory at his resurrection.

If we truly understood our position in Christ, there would no longer be finger pointing and condemnation in the church. People would no longer leave church because of the embarrassment of past sins. Furthermore, where there is no condemnation, the draw of sin loses it power.

The law is the strength of sin. Romans 7:8 says; *"For without the law, sin is dead."* If people are no longer under the law, sin loses its power.

We've been deceived by Satan to believe
just the opposite. We think if we make
people feel ashamed, they will turn from
sin and seek God. But the worse you make
people feel, the easier it is for them to run
back to their sins. It doesn't matter what it
is, the harder you push for that guilt and
shame – the farther they run away from
God. **It is the love of God that brings
people to repentance.**

Many Christians labor under the belief that
sin is just a natural part of life and it can't
always be avoided. I believe that when we
walk after the Spirit, we lose the draw
toward sin. We don't even desire to sin. It
never enters the equation because there is

fellowship with God apart from the guilt of our pasts. There is love and grace that produces righteousness – effortlessly! To be spiritually minded is life and peace.

Believing who we are in God is vital to our survival in a world of chaos. Sin has severely decayed all of creation. We are far from the original plan for mankind. There are many stumbling blocks that threaten our ability to reach our full potential. But knowing who we are in God is half the battle.

Who can tell us we aren't qualified for that promotion? Who can deny us the ability to live above the poverty line? But more than just personal growth, there is tremendous possibility for us to reach the entire world as ambassadors for Christ. Nothing can stop us from sharing the Gospel or seeing the sick healed if we truly believe what God says about us. The same power that raised Jesus from the dead is alive in us!

"The eyes of your understanding being enlightened; that ye may know what is the hope of his calling, and what the riches of the glory of his inheritance in the saints, And what is the exceeding greatness of his power to us-ward who believe, according to the working of his mighty power, Which he wrought in Christ, when he raised him

from the dead, and set him at his own right hand in the heavenly places."

Ephesians 1:18-20

This scripture is at the heart of the book you are reading. Paul is praying for the church at Ephesus that they would have the eyes of their understanding opened, meaning that they would be able to see what Christ has truly given them in the gift of salvation. Paul called what we now have *exceeding greatness.* We possess something infinitely great on the inside. Infinitely greater than our circumstances. Infinitely greater than fear or rejection or insecurity. Infinitely greater than cancer or aids. What we have on the inside is the same power that raised Jesus from the dead!

Romans 8:11 says; *"If the Spirit of him that raised up Jesus from the dead dwell in you, he that raised up Christ from the dead will also quicken your mortal bodies by his spirit that dwells in you."*

To quicken means to *spring to life*.

We have been sprung to life like a flower that blooms. The Spirit of God is alive and active in us, waiting for the opportunity to unleash God's power on a sick and dying generation.

I used to tell a testimony as a young teacher in the church. I was completely off base. I had been at the peak of my cooking career when I accepted a new cook's position at a posh Italian restaurant in Norfolk Virginia. It had been my dream job where I would be cooking authentic Italian cuisine with all locally grown ingredients. The owners were passionate and very particular about the people they hired. It was a big deal to get this job. I moved from my mom's house in Hampton (about 30 minutes away) and was on my own for the second time in life. I thought this was my chance to really become independent and successful as an adult.

Well, as the months progressed, I felt more and more out of place in my new surroundings. Work had become increasingly challenging in a way that tested my skills as a Chef. The menu was constantly changing according to the availability of fresh local fare. The bosses desired a quick learner who could juggle several orders at once. It was a long process of partially cooking something then setting it aside to cook something else. Then at the waiter's command I'd have to bring the old pan back to the fire and finish the dish. It would have been overwhelming for anyone on a busy Friday night. I was clearly in over my head.

Additionally, my new roommate was my polar opposite. He was an older Caucasian biker dude. He was very kind and opened a room in his home for me to rent. But being a single, black female always made me cautious around him. Trips from the shower back to my bedroom were always a little stressful. He had just gone through a break up with his fiancée and looked to me for friendship as well. Even though I had nothing to fear in his presence, I never quite felt at home there.

Then I received the news after a disastrous Saturday night on the sauté station: I was fired. Not long after that, I packed my things and scuttled back to mom's house feeling defeated and asking God what I was supposed to do. My faulty doctrine at the time caused me to believe that maybe God had a hand in this epic failure.

I attributed all my troubles to God's mysterious nature, his wanting to teach me a lesson through hardship. Here I was broke, unemployed, and living back home thinking God could want this for me.

The common teaching is that some of the bad things that happen to us are for a reason ordained by God. Somehow God was trying to teach me to trust and rely on Him. He was the reason I lost my job and couldn't get adjusted in Norfolk.

Many of you might agree with this thinking. Maybe something traumatic has happened and you think God was at work to tear some things out of your life as a lesson on patience, or faith, or obedience.

Well, if we always believe that God is mysteriously orchestrating every situation – even disaster, then life becomes a roller coaster. We are just trying to hang on until it's over. If we believe that God is mysterious and unpredictable, then we will always be unsure of which way to turn.

This is how faulty doctrine works. You don't have a clear idea of God's true nature because one day He is giving you good things and the next He is snatching things away. You aren't sure where you stand with Him. You're suffering for the Lord, just hoping you are doing well enough that He will finally step in and answer your prayer for help. We have been taught that it's a sign of spiritual maturity to endure hardship for the Lord.

Boy, have we missed it!

God will never deliberately cause your pain to teach you/grow you/strengthen you.

Many Christians would shut this book and walk away because this is such an ingrained teaching that I am coming against. In fact, I could fill an entire full-length book defending the statements I have just made. Still, I pray you keep reading.

Let's look at Luke 11:5-13

"And I say unto you, Ask, and it shall be given you; seek, and ye shall find; knock, and it shall be opened unto you. For every one that asks receives; and he that seeks finds; and to him that knocks it shall be opened. If a son shall ask bread of any of you that is a father, will he give him a stone? Or if he ask a fish, will he for a fish give him a serpent? Or if he shall ask an egg, will he offer him a scorpion?

If ye then, being evil, know how to give good gifts unto your children: how much more shall your heavenly Father give the Holy Spirit to them that ask him?"

It seems very clear to me that Jesus is expressing how absurd it would be to think God, or any good father, would deny his child in need.

> **The truth is that God has already offered you the answer before the problem even arrived!**

We think it's holy to suffer while waiting on a silent God. When it seems that God has gone silent it is often because we are asking Him to do what He gave us the power to do for ourselves.

We ask God for all manner of things he already appropriated in Christ. Healing and deliverance are yours. But the only way you can discover what you have is to study His Word.

For example, we want God to remove the sinful desires that torment us but the Word says in James 4:7, "Submit yourselves to God, resist the devil and he will flee."

You have the power to resist the devil for yourself. God won't fight him for you. You are much more powerful than any devil in hell. You have the Spirit of the living God on the inside. God has not left you alone!

We ask God to help us receive more faith, but Romans 12:3 says, *"For I say, through the grace given unto me, to every man that is among you, not to think of himself more highly than he ought to think; but to think soberly, according as God hath dealt to every man the measure of faith."*

When you examine this verse, Paul is saying that we have no reason to feel superior to any other believer because we have all been given the same measure of faith. No one Christian can boast in their level of faith. We can't pray to receive more faith because what we have been given is sufficient! You don't need more faith, but you do need *less* doubt and unbelief.

If we truly understood how God sees us; perfect in His sight and identical to Jesus in our spirits, we would not believe He desired to harm us for our own good. God desires to give good gifts to His children. He desires to bless us and not curse us.

We are not perfected by hardship. We are perfected by the Word of God. Once we allow the word of God to penetrate our hearts, it becomes the knowledge that will transform our minds.

"The word of God is quick and powerful, and sharper than any two-edged sword, piercing even to the dividing asunder of

*soul and spirit, and of the joints and
marrow, and is a discerner of the thoughts
and intents of the heart."*

Hebrews 4:12

> **If God wants to get your attention,
> He does so through His Word!**

Galatians 5:6 says *faith works by love.*
When God's love is demonstrated towards
us, it causes us to believe. This truth is
most evident in the lives of people in third
world countries who have virtually nothing.
When kindness is shown, it produces hope.
There is hope that their loved ones will
survive because someone came along with

food or antibiotics and met their need right in the pit of despair.

But even in less severe cases, whenever we are able to meet the needs of someone in trouble, it produces hope. And hope is what faith is made of. **When God loves us, our faith is strengthened. When we are afflicted, our faith is tested.**

"Let no man say when he is tempted, I am tempted of God: for God cannot be tempted with evil, neither tempts he any man: But every man is tempted, when he is drawn away of his own lust, and enticed. Then when lust hath conceived, it

brings forth sin: and sin, when it is finished, brings forth death. Do not err, my beloved brethren. <u>Every good gift and every perfect gift is from above</u>, and cometh down from the Father of lights, with whom is no variableness, neither shadow of turning."

James 1:13-17

God will not test us, but Satan certainly will.

Your every need is met

If God only wants to bless us, then we must address why many believers don't receive those blessings.

We must understand that what Christ did on the cross was the catalyst for every breakthrough we would ever need in life. The cross was a finished work and Jesus is seated at the right hand of the Father, (Matt. 26:64, Mark 14:62, and Luke 22:69).

Many people miss that...

If Christ is **seated** then it means He is no longer at work. He is resting just as it was on the seventh day when The Father rested.

God didn't rest because he was *pooped*! He rested because there was nothing more to be done that could make the job any better. It was perfect. Likewise, Christ's work on the cross was perfect.

What does that mean?

Everything you will ever need has been provided! 2 Peter 1:3 says; *"According as his divine power hath given unto us all things that pertain unto life and godliness, through the knowledge of him that hath called us to glory and virtue."*

(That's your cue to shout).

If you're still mulling this over in your mind it might be because many of us don't see the manifestation of this word, but I assure you - you already have it.

You are complete in your spirit. Colossians 2:9-10, *"For in you dwells all the fullness of the Godhead bodily. And you are complete in him, which is the head of all principality and power."*

There is nothing you lack because your spirit contains all the power you will ever need for breakthrough. We are three part beings. We have a physical body, a soul, and a spirit.

The spirit is the part of us that lives on forever. The soul houses our personality and drives our emotions. The spirit is unique in that it has been completely renewed after we were born again. Before salvation, there was an unclean spirit in us that only desired to do evil continually. That old man was crucified with Christ and we received a new spirit that is identical to God. (Romans 6:8).

If we can really comprehend the spirit within us, we can start to believe what God says about us. We are righteous. We are mighty. We are blessed.

We also have received the Holy Spirit.

2 Corinthians 1:22; *"He has sealed us and given the earnest [promise] of the Holy Spirit in our hearts."*

Our spirit is sealed with the Holy Spirit. This is vital because in the Spirit there is supernatural ability given to every believer.

You also have the fruit of the Spirit that is always in season on the inside of you. There is constantly love, joy, peace, longsuffering, gentleness, goodness, faith, meekness, and temperance alive in you.

Some believe that the fruit is something to grow into. We think we have to practice these things and then somehow they will manifest... *Fake it till you make it.*

Now while that method might work, for a little while, some days will be harder than others. People will irritate you and you won't always respond in love. You will be running late and lose your patience in traffic. *There is no way to always demonstrate the fruit of the Spirit, right?*

Well, if we change our perspective and just believe we already have the ability in us, we might surprise ourselves.

> **It's harder to get something you don't have than to draw from something that's already there.**

The fruit of the Spirit is always in season. That fruit just needs to be drawn out. First we must accept that it already exists in the spiritual realm. Then we must renew our minds to the Word of God so that we can exhibit that fruit in the natural realm.

Not only do we have this completeness in our spirit, lacking nothing, but we also have creative genius on the inside. There is a part of your brain that was made to produce nothing but ideas. There are dormant visions in you that could completely eradicate poverty in your life. I tell you the truth, if you are in Christ you are lacking nothing!

We have the mind of Christ

"For who hath known the mind of the Lord, that he may instruct him? But we have the mind of Christ." 1 Corinthians 2:16

"You have an unction from the Holy One, and you know all things." 1 John 2:20.

Yes... YOU have been given the mind of Christ. You know all things. Now I'm sure those wheels are turning in you r brain because there is a major disconnect between what God's Word says about us and what we perceive.

You are probably thinking; *"How can I know all things when I can hardly remember what happened yesterday?"*

Remember principle #2 - We must first accept what the Word says about us then draw out those qualities by renewing our minds.

God desires for you to prosper in all areas of your life. There are latent gifts, talents, and creativity on the inside of you. There is a business, a bestseller, or a million-dollar idea just waiting to be pulled out. The very purpose for your existence is waiting to be discovered. The mind we've been given already knows what to do.

> **To understand what God has given us, we have to walk after the spirit.**

What does it mean to walk after the spirit?

Walking after the spirit is allowing the things of God to have more influence on your thinking and actions than the things of the world.

The world is opposed to the things of God. Everything God established is countered by something in the natural world. We as human beings are tethered between years of worldly, carnal teaching and the new life we have in Christ. To many new believers, the Bible is mysterious and often confusing.

There is only one way to transition from the carnal way of thinking, (which is fixed on the 5 senses) to thinking the way God thinks; we must have more faith in His word than we have in the world around us.

We must no longer see the world by what our 5 senses perceive because our senses only tell half the story. We are not just a physical body, aimlessly roaming the earth. We are also spirit. There is an entire composition that cannot be seen with the natural eye. However just as sound waves flow through the air undetected by our ears, so does the spiritual realm. Your senses may not pick up on them, but they do exist.

God is telling us to walk according to what is true in the spiritual realm because that is where your power can be found.

In the world, seeing is believing but with God, *believing is seeing.*

Once opened, our spiritual eyes can see far more than our natural eyes. We are able to see ourselves how God sees us. We are able to imagine ourselves doing incredible things. Suddenly, we are doing the greater works Jesus spoke of in John 14:12 because we understand that He has made miracles available to us today.

You certainly have the Mind of Christ, but it requires fine tuning like a radio dial. The junk and clutter of the world must be swept away so that the *God signal* can be heard loud and clear. This is accomplished by habitually reading God's Word until it becomes 3 dimensional in your life.

"I beseech you therefore, brethren, by the mercies of God, that you present your bodies a living sacrifice, holy, acceptable unto God, which is your reasonable service. And be not conformed to this world: but be ye transformed by the renewing of your mind, that you may prove what is that good, and acceptable, and perfect, will of God."

Romans 12:1-2

As we slowly start to tear down the false wisdom of the world and begin to embrace

God's wisdom, we will see greater expressions of His blessings in the natural realm.

Can you believe that your sins are forgiven, that you have the same spirit as Christ himself, and that you have the mind of Christ? Knowing who you are in Him makes you unstoppable!

#3

We must cooperate with the ministry of the Holy Spirit

So we have established that we have the mind of Christ. This mind has given us spiritual insight. God has given us yet another blessing help us navigate this life. We have been given the Holy Spirit and we must rely on him to give understanding.

1 Corinthians 2:12, "What we have received is not the spirit of the world, but the Spirit who is from God, so that we may understand what God has freely given us."

When is the last time you sought the counsel of the Holy Spirit on a major decision? It is by the Spirit of God in us that we can discern the mysteries of life. Many of us are walking with God and we find ourselves still making poor decisions. Perhaps you find yourself in a difficult marriage and you don't know what to do. Maybe you keep going back to the same destructive patterns even though you've been praying for a different path. Many times we find ourselves *saved and stuck*.

The Holy Spirit has come to be our Helper. Some look upon the Holy Spirit as the moral compass. From childhood, we are taught to let our conscience be our guide. Many consider the Holy Spirit to be their inner conscience, but this is false. We are born with a sense of morality. That is a characteristic of God's nature imparted to us because we are born in His image.

The Holy Spirit is not your conscience, however He does speak to us when we contemplate our actions. He is that still, small voice. The Holy Spirit is your guide. The key is to be sensitive to what your guide is saying.

We may not always make the right choices just because we have become sensitive to the Holy Spirit. We will still make mistakes or say the wrong thing at times. The primary role of the Holy Spirit is to remind us of God's desire for us.

I can remember a time when I was a child. I had been waiting in the car for my mother to pick up a few things at the drugstore. I was fiddling with the radio when I glanced into my rearview window. There was an elderly woman hobbling with a cane in one hand. I could tell she was struggling to make the seemingly short trip from her car to the door. Suddenly, I felt a nudge to get out of the car and help her into the store. At that moment, I began telling myself why it wasn't a good idea to help her. I imagined this woman feeling offended by my attempt to help her. I also became consumed with my own self-consciousness about approaching strangers.

After all my self-talk, I had decided to stay in the car instead of helping this elderly woman and then my mom sprang into view.

I sat watching my mother cheerfully usher the woman into the store. I began to feel crummy for being so selfish.

When my mother returned to the car, I said; "I was supposed to help that lady." I sunk lower in my seat and continued, "I heard God telling me to help her but I didn't."

Let this be an illustration that the Holy Spirit is speaking all the time. He was the nudge that said I should help someone in need, but it was ultimately my choice to either follow that instruction or follow my own mind.

We always have a choice. I learned two things that day with my mom:

> **1. If you don't go, God will send someone else.**

> **2. We never know how our obedience to the Holy Spirit is going to positively affect someone else.**

We get the nudge from the Holy Spirit to do something nice and it might seem so inconsequential to us, but for someone, you might be the very thing they needed to reinforce that God is real. We never know the inner turmoil someone might be facing and God just wants to use us to remind them that they are not alone.

The Holy Spirit also has another important role. He gives understanding of the mysteries of God.

1 Corinthians 2:10-13 says; "The Spirit searches all things, even the deep things of God.

For who knows a person's thoughts except their own spirit within them? In the same

*way no one knows the thoughts of God
except the Spirit of God.*

*What we have received is not the spirit of
the world, but the Spirit who is from God,
so that we may understand what God has
freely given us.*

*This is what we speak, not in words taught
us by human wisdom but in words taught
by the Spirit, explaining spiritual realities
with Spirit-taught words."*

**The first step on the journey of unlocking
those mysteries is by *praying in the Spirit*.**

It's just plain unfortunate that certain
churches do not embrace speaking in

tongues. My fathers in the faith grew up in a generation that thought speaking in tongues was from the devil! *Can you imagine?* The modern thinking isn't as harsh as it was then. Still, there is not enough teaching on the subject.

The Pentecostal Christians are big on "tongue talking" but the teaching is also paired with the idea that you have to first be free of any sin before you can speak in tongues. The belief is that your sin will prevent the Spirit from moving. Then once you let the Spirit come, the tongues just come over you.

For others, being in the Spirit is like a high point in the service when the tongues come out uncontrollably. It is a spectacle. People are gyrating and falling to the floor while others dance or run around.

It's not my intention to offend if you come from a Pentecostal background. But let me emphasize that the ministry of the Holy Spirit is much deeper than just a high time in praise.

I grew up as a Baptist and never experienced a great deal of teaching on this subject. People occasionally spoke in tongues and sometimes others would offer an interpretation. Still, I didn't really know what it was about. I learned a little something about tongues through a teaching tape from a well-known evangelist at the time. I was introduced to the Baptism of the Holy Spirit at the age of fourteen.

Speaking in tongues is not just something that comes over us when the feeling is right. We put our faith in action by opening our mouths and beginning to speak. The Holy Spirit will not force the words out of your mouth. Once you receive the Baptism of the Holy Spirit, you are free to speak in tongues whenever you want to. You can speak in tongues at will.

> **Speaking in tongues, also called *Praying in the Spirit*, is perfect communication between us and God.**

Essentially, it is a prayer language in which your spirit communicates with God without the hindrances of your flesh to mix your prayer with doubt and unbelief.

Often times when we pray in English, we spend most of the time telling God how big our problems are. But when we pray in the Spirit, we are standing in agreement with God's Word in prayer. Our spirit begins to echo what the Word of God says instead of the bad report of the enemy.

We NEED the Baptism of the Holy Spirit.

Praying in tongues equips us for the spiritual battle we are constantly facing. That time in prayer gives us an advantage over the enemy as we travel through our day. For most of us, that time in prayer is the difference between keeping our cool under stress and having a total meltdown!

The baptism of the Holy Spirit is different from the water baptism you experience after being born again. Water baptism is simply an outward, physical expression of what has already happened on the inside.

Water baptism symbolizes the death of your old sinful man and the birth of the new man who is like Jesus, (Col. 2:12).

However, when you are baptized in the Holy Spirit, you are receiving **power**. Now don't be mistaken, we have all received the Holy Spirit at the point of salvation.

"In whom ye also trusted, after that ye heard the word of truth, the gospel of your salvation: in whom also after that ye believed, ye were sealed with that Holy Spirit of promise" Ephesians 1:13

We were sealed with the Spirit at salvation, but the **baptism** endows us with the *power* of the Holy Spirit. And this power is typically signified by speaking in tongues.

You can read more about this encounter in Acts 2 at the day of Pentecost.

Acts 10:44-46,"While Peter yet spake these words, the Holy Ghost fell on all them which heard the word. And they of the circumcision which believed were astonished, as many as came with Peter, because that on the Gentiles also was poured out the gift of the Holy Ghost. For they heard them speak with tongues, and magnify God."

Here we see Peter baptizing in the Holy Spirit at Caesarea. The rest of the chapter continues with the people asking for water baptism only after they received the baptism of the Holy Spirit, further identifying this as a separate act.

We can reap tremendous benefits of having the baptism of the Holy Spirit.

It is very difficult to be an over-comer without the baptism of the Holy Spirit. It is like fighting a battle with only half your armor. Lacking this power leaves you vulnerable to the enemy. Praying in the Spirit – or praying in tongues is the secret weapon in our arsenal. When we pray in tongues, the Holy Spirit is praying with us, revealing mysteries to us, interceding for us, and bringing peace to our hearts. With the Spirit, we are communing with God on a much deeper level.

"But ye shall receive power, after that the Holy Ghost is come upon you: and ye shall be witnesses unto me both in Jerusalem, and in all Judaea, and in Samaria, and unto the uttermost part of the earth." Acts 1:8

The Greek word for power is *Dunamis*. This word is the root for dynamite but it is more complex than that. *Dunamis* power is *supernatural ability.* It is the kind of ability believers need to fight against the snares of the enemy.

Do you desire to be filled with the Holy Spirit? Well, just as when you received Jesus as Lord and Savior by faith, you receive this baptism by faith. Let's pray a simple prayer now and ask God to fill you with his Holy Spirit:

Lord,

I thank you for the love that you have shown toward us in your son Jesus Christ. Thank you for a changed heart that is open to accept who you say that I am.

Lord, I ask you now to fill me with your Holy Spirit. I open the door and I welcome your power to come into me.

I thank you and praise you for your precious Holy Spirit.

Amen.

Now begin thanking God out loud with your mouth. Lift your hands and continue praising God. Then let your outward and vocal praise flow out in tongues. It may feel awkward or forced at first but remember this is an act of faith. Believe that God has truly filled you. You may not feel anything miraculous happen when you receive the baptism, but there is a wonderful change happening on the inside. For some, the manifestation of tongues doesn't come instantly, but continue to vocally worship the Lord and it will come.

Once you get into the practice of praying in the Spirit, it will transform you from the inside out. The Holy Spirit is our guide to all the things we have been seeking. Let him be your guide and many things will start to become clear.

Building upon the Foundation

At this point, you have an adequate launching pad for deeper study. It is my prayer that you continue uncovering what has previously been hidden from you. I often ask myself why more churches aren't teaching these things. I have a few theories but more importantly, I am thankful for the teachers God has sent me and for the opportunity to share these truths with others. They have certainly changed my life and renewed my relationship with our Lord and Savior. As you continue to meditate on the three principles discussed in this book, you will begin that all important process of renewing your mind.

Now that you have a foundation from which to build on, let's examine some common areas where Christians who don't have these principles struggle.

Taking Authority

Many of us believe what the Word says about prosperity, health, and peace but we seldom see these things in real life and it causes a barrier between us and God. We subconsciously think, *well either God's a liar or something is wrong with me!*

Well...God is not a liar.

"For all the promises of God in him are yea, and in him Amen, unto the glory of God by us."

2 Corinthians 1:20.

God is not unpredictable and God is not withholding blessings from you until you earn them with your good behavior.

Start to meditate on the goodness of God and His promises. Let them become rooted in your heart so that whenever a challenge comes it will be like a siren going off in your mind. You will instantly recognize fear and doubt and unbelief and cast it down!

"For the weapons of our warfare are not carnal, but mighty through God to the pulling down of strong holds; Casting down imaginations, and every **high thing that exalts itself against the knowledge of God, and bringing into captivity every thought to the obedience of Christ."**

2 Corinthians 10:4-5

We are constantly fighting against unbelief! Let nothing sway your from your faith in God to do exactly what He said He would do. If we aren't seeing the blessings He promised it is because we don't know how to get them.

We can have everything the Word says we can have.

Peace

Everyone wants peace. So why do some seek it, pray for it, will it to come but still can't find it? Often times a person who doesn't experience peace is too busy looking at what is wrong all the time. Whatever we give the most attention to will become magnified in our minds.

I once saw a street magician perform a simple card trick for a crowd of onlookers. He asked the crowd to pay close attention.

Then he performed some pretty clever illusions. Everyone was amazed by his sleight of hand and applauded. When he was done, he smirked then asked; *"Now did anyone notice the giant kangaroo that just hopped by us?"*

The entire crowd laughed in bewilderment because every one of them were so focused on the card tricks that something so strange had never even registered in their minds.

I love this illustration because there is something hard wired in us to naturally phase out those things that don't matter in order to give our full attention to something else. It's the same way you can lose a pair of sunglasses as soon as you stop consciously keeping track of them.

I believe that Adam and Eve had singular focus before the fall. Their only focus was their relationship with God. Genesis 3:7 says their eyes were opened and they suddenly knew they were naked.

Now, I don't particularly believe that their physical eyes were completely closed up until this time. I believe it was the eyes of their understanding. They no longer were just aware of the goodness of God but also had new awareness to sin and evil.

We have all taken our minds and hearts off God at one time or another.

> **Experiencing peace begins with putting the focus back on the things of God.**

That is why Paul said to be carnally minded is death, but to be spiritually minded is life and peace, (Romans 8:6). When we focus our attention on what we have in the spirit, it is magnified greater than what's wrong. Having peace (or any other fruit of the spirit) is a matter of choice! Remember that the fruit of the Spirit is always alive in you.

.

Health

Good health is ours because it was bought and purchased at the cross. Christ destroyed the curse of sin and death. He took our sickness and diseases. By His stripes we **were** healed, (2 Peter 2:24). It is no longer present tense, (as it was written in Isaiah 53:5), but *past* tense because it is already done. If you aren't experiencing good health, it is not because you are still waiting on God to heal. **It is already done.**

Receive what He did by faith and speak to your body to be well in Jesus name!

Did you know that your words have power? Jesus spoke to a barren fig tree in Mark 11. It bore no fruit so he cursed it and it later withered and died. It was done by the very words of his mouth. The disciples were amazed. So Jesus used this as a teaching tool. He said have faith in God.

"That whosoever shall say unto this mountain, Be thou removed, and be thou cast into the sea; and shall not doubt in his heart, but shall believe that those things which he saith shall come to pass; he shall have whatsoever he saith. Therefore I say

unto you, What things soever ye desire, when ye pray, believe that ye receive them, and ye shall have them."

Mark 11:23-24

You can speak to your situation and see things change. Notice here that Jesus didn't say that if you beg and plead with God – the mountain would be removed. No.

He also didn't say to strap on your burdens and climb the rough side of the mountain.

He placed the power squarely in your hands to overcome!

> **It is the Word of God mixed with your faith that causes things to change.**

Some Christians will take this to mean that we are supposed to *'name it and claim it'* for fancy cars, a new supermodel wife/husband, and winning lottery tickets!

Uh...Sorry.

God is not going to help you party like a rock star. He has empowered us to claim what is *already* ours in the spirit. The Word is full of promises that we need to declare over our families, our physical bodies, and our finances. If what you desire lines up with scripture, then speak those verses over your life. Believe that you can have whatever you say, and it will come to pass as the Word promises.

Your physical body responds to what you think and feel. If you think sick, you will speak sick, and you will feel sick. The same applies to depression, anxiety, fear, and all manner of negativity.

It's time to stop surrendering to whatever diagnosis the Doctor gives. I can't tell you how many times doctors have made mistakes. The medical profession is valid, yes. But common practice for doctors is to give you the worst case scenario because they are trying to avoid a malpractice suit if things go badly for you. They will recommend blood tests and screenings as a precaution, but we spend the days and weeks after the test thinking we are at death's door. We can actually make ourselves feel sicker after a visit from the doctor.

That kind of gloom and doom thinking is far from the victory Christ promised we could have.

I think we sometimes forget that the body is not the sum total of our being. The body is simply a tool, a vessel to carry out a purpose. In fact, if we lose this mortal body, we do not cease, but live on in the presence of the Lord as a spirit. *Therefore, where is the greater power: In the body or the inner man?* **Greater is he that is in you!**

Your body must submit to your command. What tool is greater than the person using it? Even a sophisticated computer is only as smart as the person at the keyboard. Let your body be a tool to carry out your purpose. Bring it under submission to the authority that is within you.

Some of you might be experiencing a serious health battle. Please don't take my words as insensitivity to your plight. I am fully confident that healing is available to you right this moment. But for those who have been sick a long time, it might take longer to see your healing because you have been *thinking sick* for so long.

You must renew your mind. Review Truth #2 again until you see yourself the way God sees you – complete in Him!

Prosperity

Poverty is a part of the curse. Many people don't associate poverty with sin, but anything that causes us to live apart from the blessings of God is not of Him. God is not the author of poverty. Some have taken to believing that there is great honor in a life of poverty; that there is a special blessing for those who have very little. But if I am in line at social services and you are right behind me, how can you help meet my need?

Others say that there are many ways to be a blessing - and that is true. But we all know there is not a person alive who has no need for money. Money is not an evil thing to be avoided.

If we hare honest, it is usually someone without much money who declares money to be evil. I have never heard a rich person complain that money is evil. Unfortunately, poor people spend way too much time thinking of how they can find more money to survive. Their thought life is unbalanced and so money becomes the villain.

1 Timothy 6:10, "For the love of money is the root of all kinds of evil. And some people, craving money, have wandered from the true faith and pierced themselves with many sorrows."

Some Christians are afraid to admit they need money to live. As if saying that you need more money is a sin. God already knows what you have need of. He also knows you have bills to pay just like everyone else. This idea that you don't need money because you can be rich in spirit doesn't go over well with the electric company. Let's all just drop the pious façade and accept that money is a part of life on earth.

Luke 11:13, "If ye then, being evil, know how to give good gifts unto your children: how much more shall your heavenly Father give the Holy Spirit to them that ask him?"

God is not stingy! *Do you think He would live in a city paved with gold and only give you enough to get by? Is that love?* No. When you are blessed, it blesses your Father in Heaven. He wants to see his children prosper.

> **The best part about prosperity is that it puts you in a position to bless someone else.**

Being prosperous is not about you, but about being a blessing to someone else.

Money is a seed and it needs to be scattered. As believers, we ought to seek to be a blessing wherever we see a need.

The world system dictates that when you only have a little you must hold onto it with tight fists. But in God's system, give even out of your little bit and it returns to you 10, 20, 30, or 100 times over. Now, the key here is not to give an offering this Sunday and expect a check for $10,000 to be in the mail on Monday.

God designed a natural law that dictates seed, time, and then harvest. It takes *time* for a seed to grow and for a harvest to be reaped. **But keep sowing seed and you will see a continual harvest in your life.** Your needs will be met in a greater way and your ability to bless others will increase as well.

After all, it is the sacrifice God honors. God doesn't need your money – but money is the easiest way to be a blessing to someone. You could only have $5.00 to your name, but giving half of it away shows that you are putting faith in God to return it 10, 20, or 100 times over what you gave. **Giving is an act of faith.**

We live a very blessed life here in America because even our poorest are doing a great deal better than those in Third World Countries. It is a fallacy to think that your prosperity will come in the form of a McMansion on a hill with a Bently and a Beemer in the drive. We liken God to a magic genie in a bottle that you rub just right.

Instead, consider prosperity as living well and giving freely out of your abundance. Imagine working a job that doesn't feel like work but serves the Kingdom and pays you well for doing something you enjoy. Prosperity is having more than enough for you and your family. Prosperity is having so much that you can't give it away fast enough before more comes flowing in. God can get glory from a life like that.

Conclusion

Attaining the abundant life God promised is not nearly as hard as we have been taught. It honestly comes down to making the Word of God top priority in your life, letting His word be the final authority in all your decision making. If God has called you blessed, then you are blessed!

You must believe what He says about you – that you have the same righteousness as Jesus by His spirit and you have the mind of

Christ. This new identity makes you unshakable in the face of adversity.

Recognize that you are not alone in this life. You have a Helper in the Holy Spirit! So pray in the Spirit daily to let the Lord lead you as you pursue the purpose that is within you.

This great gift of salvation was poured out on mankind for one reason: So that we would be free to worship Him. All that God has ever wanted was to commune with you. So now that sin and false teachings are no longer holding you hostage - worship Him! Walk with Him. Talk with

Him. Be free to Love God, letting Him love you.

Final Note

I pray that you truly receive every spiritual blessing that God has richly provided in His son Jesus Christ who is the propitiation for our sins. May you walk in true righteousness and holiness all the days of your life. Amen.